THE INFINITESIMALS

Also by Laura Kasischke

ASISCHKE

THE INFINITESIMALS

Copper Canyon Press
Port Townsend, Washington

Cover art: Joel James Devlin, *Vectors*, 2012. Photography, medium format.

Copper Canyon Press is in residence at Fort Worden State Park in Port Townsend, Washington, under the auspices of Centrum. Centrum is a gathering place for artists and creative thinkers from around the world, students of all ages and backgrounds, and audiences seeking extraordinary cultural enrichment.

LIBRARY OF CONGRESS CATALOGING-IN-PUBLICATION DATA

Kasischke, Laura, 1961–
[Poems. Selections]
The Infinitesimals / Laura Kasischke.
  pages   cm
ISBN 978-1-55659-466-3 (paperback)
I. Title.
PS3561.A6993A6 2014
811'.54—dc23
        2013050811

9 8 7 6 5 4 3 2 FIRST PRINTING

COPPER CANYON PRESS
Post Office Box 271
Port Townsend, Washington 98368

www.coppercanyonpress.org

for Bill, Lucy & Jack Abernethy

They are neither finite quantities nor quantities infinitely small, nor yet nothing. May we not call them the ghosts of departed quantities?

George Berkeley

Contents

ONE

Outside Are the Dogs and the Sorcerers

TWO

At the End of the Text, a Small Bestial Form

THREE

That Men Should Kill One Another

FOUR

A Dog, About to Pounce, Looks Back

THE INFINITESIMALS

ONE

Outside Are the Dogs and the Sorcerers

You've Come Back to Me

for G

A small thing crawling toward me
across this dark lawn. Bright
eyes the only thing I'm sure I see.

You've come back to me,
haven't you, my sweet? From
long ago, and very far. Through

crawling dark, my sweet, you've
come back to me, have you? Even
smaller this time than the stars.

The Two Witnesses

When I saw your body in the world
I knew exactly who you were, and I
stared at you
as you stared at me, both
of us crawling in through the other's
eyes, depositing, then
leaving.

You were the one in the bed
getting ready to leave—incurable
woman like a broken
wing
tucked beneath
a sheet.

I was the volunteer girl

for a few hours the
day you died.

You were the woman I would be.

I was the girl you were.

And then

seated at the train window:
Landscape.
Damp faces.
Both of us witness
to everything.

Who

Who are these elders
in their white robes? These
females and males? These
royals and ruled? Who

are these children? This woman beside me? This
magician, this priest, this meat in this soup, this
utter conundrum—what

is it, and where did it come from?

O Kepler, O Newton, O Darwin, O Driesch.
What machinery all night, and all day
what dream?

And where is my father? I asked and I asked—but I

was no more than the windmill asking
questions of its own
shadow on the grass.

He was never here, they told me. Your
father is not in his bed and not in his grave. No one
has ever lived here
who answered to your father's name.

I insisted. I begged. I tore my hair. They
gave me sad expressions, then

tea, then pills, then
exasperation. *We're*

sorry, but you're
terribly mistaken.

But, having come to visit my father, I
knelt down in the desert and parted the sands
to search for the path on my knees and hands.
I drank from the mirage

of the pond for an answer until,
finally, the water lilies asked me:

Who was your father?

as they floated there
all girlish laughter and waxen hands, making
and remaking themselves without fathers
out of water and air.

In This Order

A tail, a torso, a tiny face.
A longing, a journey, a deep belief.
A spawning, a fissioning, a bit of tissue
anchored to a psyche,
stitched to a wish.
Watery. Irony. Memory. My
mother, my face, and then

the last thing
she'd ever see, and then
the last words
I'd hear her say: *You're*
killing me.

Hurry

You cannot cross this border
without your name. *Think
harder*, the stone says
as it slips into the milk, that

great pale vat out of which
my mother selected
the sound of it
from the same silence
that surrounds me now.

Pen in hand. Marble statue
standing at the center
of the great museum

whispering, whispering, without
needing to move her lips:

Listen.

I try, but I
can't hear it.

Hurry.

The old man
with tears in his eyes
watches his old brother hobble
to the men's room at McDonald's.

Mushrooms

Like silent naked monks huddled
around an old tree stump, having
spun themselves in the night
out of thought and nothingness—

And God so pleased with their silence
He grants them teeth and tongues.

Like us.

How long have you been gone?
A child's hot tears on my bare arms.

The Invisible Passenger

Between row 12 and row 14, there
are, on this plane, no seats. This

engineering feat of
gravity and wings, which
flies on superstition, irrationality. The calm

has been printed on my ticket:

Doe and fawn
in a grove below us, her
soul crawling in and out of my clothes.

While, in a roofless theater, a magic act
is performed for children
by an invisible man.

Like the mess

of a cake that I once
baked for my father—

damp, awful, crumbling layers.
Soggy church bell on a plate.

And my father's dentures, lost
(all his teeth
pulled out
as a young man
by a military dentist im-
patient to send him

on his way), and

my father's smile anyway.

This Is Not a Poem/Fairy Tale

Sixteen years ago in northern Michigan, somewhere in the Huron National Forest, a man and a woman from a nearby town pulled over to the shoulder of the road, took their two-year-old son, asleep, out of the backseat, walked with him into the woods a mile or so, and set him down.

It was still light enough for them to find their way back to their car. God help us, they went home.

These people. Drugs were involved, we must suppose. Some kind of profound stupidity made greater with desperation. (Although it isn't possible to have sympathy for them, one still searches for some explanation.)

Did they sleep that night? Were they startled when the phone by the bedside rang?

Well, they confessed the whole thing the next day after the child was found walking ("toddling," the finder called it) along that shoulder of the road. A policeman recognized him from his own child's day-care center. And he was a "smart little guy. He knew his name." This much was in the paper.

Everything else you have to imagine for yourself in order to survive, as he did. In order to survive it, you have to imagine it every day. When you lie down to go to sleep, and when you wake. But, in between—

In between, your mind is full of trees.
And it's quite dark despite the moon.
But this summer's been a warm one.
And someone tied your tiny shoes for you.

How New a Summer Night

Windows in prisons.
Plastic trees.
Taxidermied birds. How

new a summer night seems
when you're eighteen.
No such thing as fate, as
in the bedroom
your mother folds
your father's undershirts. When

last we met, you and I, we
were in my dream, and still
the sun managed
to penetrate the depths. We

stood around in silence, as if underwater. Your
feet were in cement, but I was free to leave. Do

you remember
how you tried
to cling to me?

But, if I learned one thing from Red Cross that
summer, it was
that you must shake off
the one who'd hold you under.

Remember how, above you, that
membrane closed itself
so smoothly after me?

That Men Should Kill One Another

It is the bread that will not be baked.
The bread that rises and continues to rise.
It is the recital performed every night—
little girl
in a snowstorm
in an empty auditorium. Not the soldier

on a horse, bearing
a skull on a pole. No, it is the way

I call your name, many
years too late, just

your dark omnipresence now as it stretches
from one edge of the everything to the next.

The First Trumpet

In a bedroom down the road
some boy practiced taps
so slowly his slow tune
became a single note.

He was the Understander.
He was the Knower.
I was the village on the hillside
hastily nailing its doors closed.

He was my father in the driveway
refusing me the keys. Saying
nothing. Holding. Holding. I

was the exasperated girl in the top cut too low.
There was a party.
I wanted to go.

He was the army holding
that hillside. He
was that army's wounded soldiers
crawling home:
No.

At the End of the Text, a Small Bestial Form

This is the glimpse of the god you were never supposed to get.
Like the fox slipping into the thicket.
Like the thief in the night outside the window. The cool
gray dorsal fin in the distance. Invisible
mountain briefly visible through the mist
formed of love and guilt.

And the stranger's face hidden in the family picture. The one

imagining her freedom, like

the butterfly blown against the fence
in her best yellow dress
by the softest breeze of summer:

To have loved
and to have suffered. To have waited
for nothing, and for nothing to have come.

And the water like sleek black fur combed back that afternoon:

The young lovers rowed a boat. The boy
reeled in a fish. The husband
smiled, raising
a toast.

While the children grew anxious
for dinner. While something
struggled under the water,
bound by ropes.
And the warm milk dribbled down the sick man's chin.

And the wife, the mother, the daughter, the hostess, and those
few people on Earth she would ever wish were dead
were the ones she loved the most.

The Emptying of the Censers

And operated on her brain.
And moved around the very
stones of that foundation.
And poured fire into a lake.
And then stood by
whistling at the sky. *Bad
news, I'm afraid. Sit
down if you like.*

Later, I found her
in the farthest North. Five
thousand miles of train
tracks away, wearing
a black cap lined
with stars and planets, at
the vastest edge
of that northern forest
where the question
of distance
is answered by time. She

did not look surprised. *I*

*wasn't expecting you
so late,* she said, her
words set to music:

motherhood, that
grand opera
staged in a cave.

Never look at me again, she said, and
tightened the comet's tail under
her chin as she hurried away.

Canto One

Halfway. A dark
closet opened. Cables
that should have been buried lying, instead, on the lawn.

And then a muttering crowd. I recognized each one:
A sneer. A cry. That same
student, eternally
yawning and rolling her eyes. And

one guy I barely knew, and knew too well: his

awful smile
and wink.
Apparently
he'd never died.
Nor had I.
Just my high heels stuck in mud.
And these days you can find

anyone with Google. He's
a lawyer in Houston now.
I've seen his profile, along

with an extraordinary X-ray of my chest
held up to a dirty window:
that kind of light, if

you can call that light.

Every manner of cliché: the whole
reason for cliché. To say

I was twenty-one and in New York:
sparkling clutch purse full of change,
and a mirror full of me. Could

I ever have been so stupid? ("You

think these things only happen
to people who are not you?") *Don't*

touch me, don't touch me, the princess
muttered as they touched her.

Afterward, so many years
had passed between
me, and me. I thought forgotten: all of it.
Until, slowly, *she* appeared

in a housedress, still on her knees, her
face still gray, still
the young mother who stuck
her head in an oven. Nearly

twenty years younger than I am today. I thought
what could such a shade have to say? She said:

What difference does it make?

Her blinding mind.
I stepped toward it.
To unwind it.
She rolled her eyes.
She said, So
you followed me this far, Laura. Good
for you. You've

come to the right
place to die.

Shit, I thought. Oh God. They've
not sent Virgil to me, they've
sent the poet of no way out. They've
sent the poet of how to stay. She

stood where feet would be but blood had pooled instead.

Whose blood, I asked. She smiled. She said, Whose
shoes?

I froze.
How did she know?
She said, Your

little friend is here. I said, No, no, that was so
long ago. I told
her that I had a husband now, a son. I said
it's not that I forgot, but I—

And then I saw
myself

as a snapshot of a statue of a woman saying
certain things forever. But

you, she said, and I
knew where it was we were going next:
darkest hour of the night
could just as easily be
in hell or paradise, like

the alchemist's black and bleeding fingers in a basin, or
his rubber gloves, and
an infant, a ribbon, a toy I used to play with
bearing and baring a dead child's face.

Sheesh, I said, awake. *What*

food or drink or drug
this time did I take? But

it had followed me

out of the dream: Twisted

fellow on a cross in a cathedral on Amsterdam.
Or that diner on Broadway with
the steamy windows where
he and I divvied it up with our friend.

Barbed Wire

From where we stood on the other side
of the barbed-wire fence
we could see

a child asleep in forget-me-nots, like
the gentle senility
of that first summer

before the wheelchair
and the screaming

back when the birds
conversed in human words
and every nurse was your mother returned
with her sweet cup

of thankfulness

before the child
on the other side
of that barbed wire
woke from the nap, stood up, looked

around, panicked,
and began to run
with arms outstretched toward us.

Beast of the Sea

When I realized that I was no longer weighing down the boat.
That someone had built a throne
for me out of coral and abalone.
That the walls were dissolving, like a final

joy suppressed forever: the opening
and closing
of the mouth
of my angelic sister, her

hooves still damp from wading in those waters, whispering.
Then I realized that I was no longer weighing down the boat.
That someone had built a throne
for me out of coral and—

To Do

The executioner smokes a cigarette
with his coffee
in the morning.
In his lap, his good dark hood.
At his feet, a happy dog. While

someone on the other side of this amnesia
keeps calling and calling to me: *Laura, you*

forgot to turn the fire off
beneath the pan. Blow
the candle out. Pay
the paperboy, mail the card. Forgot
eye contact. And
I love you. And

to tie the boat to the dock. Forgot

to explain again before
you dropped him off
where you'd pick him up. To

unbegrudge it, another
plate, another cup, another kiss, another—

To burn the journal, tell the secret, tuck
the blanket under his legs so it would not, in the wheels
of the wheelchair, get stuck. Smooth

what hair was left on his head with a gentle hand. Speak
louder. Crouch

down. Eye
contact. White
flower. To turn

the television toward your stepmother
whether she could see it or not. To

explain it
again and again, and
once more to the shattered
former third-grade teacher

you vowed to visit: who
you were and why you'd come. Smile

at the receptionist, teach
yourself to breathe, and
someone, *someone*

please tell my husband,
remind my son...

Perspective

Like the lake turned to
steel by the twilit
sky. Like
the Flood in the toilet
to the housefly.
Like the sheet
thrown over

the secret love. Like
the sheet thrown over
the blood on the rug.

Or the pages
of the novel
scattered by the wind:
the end
at the beginning
in the middle again.

And the sudden sense.
The polished lens.
The revision
revisioned, as if
as if.

As if
the secret—
had you told me when:
who I thought
we were, every-
where we went.

Hair

A stranger in the house, but not even the stranger—

The stranger's shadow
Cast across the couch
Like bereavement and disease
And the birdbath filled with tears
And the birds—

The oblivious birds

And the girls—

The treacherous girls
Playing roulette in a barn somewhere
Wearing my old dresses
My ruined shoes
My poisonous roses

And my tombstone heaped with air
And the damp paperbacks
And the fountain clogged with moss
And the sink, full of hair

The Second Trumpet

One day in August I went
to the lobby of the hospital to listen.
One icy night in February
I drove my car into a ditch.
Once, I saw a dog in traffic, and then

the child running after it.

And after the funeral.
And just before the diagnosis.
And when
the phone call did not come
but I did not yet know what that meant.

Each time, expecting trumpets, I
received silence instead.
Expecting angels, tongues
on a slaughterhouse floor. At
the bottom of a filthy cage, their
feathers, silence, and a smell

like a classroom full of children's
sweaters, but which
might have been adrenaline.
Something glandular.
Something chemical.

It always lasted
half an hour, and then—

TWO

At the End of the Text, a Small Bestial Form

Beast of the Sea

This morning the shadow of a flag
spreads its dark picnic blanket
out across the grass, and then
snatches it back.

Something nascent in the dangling willow branches.
Something flickering, whispering, like a loose
heart at the center of that tree. Quiet

squirming toward alteration in the womb.
The bud, the grave, the cocoon. In

the fist of a child
emerging from the sea
a snake, or a balloon. The sad unrealized ambitions
that our fathers kept to themselves. The love
poems our mothers never wrote.

Let this vengeance be for them.

Boy in Park

Small boy running through the center of the park, un-
zipping summer straight down the middle as he runs until
all the small boys come tumbling out. All

the small boys pouring from the world's fissure into
the world: My

father with a ball and bat. My
husband with a wooden gun. My son in
a cowboy hat. Their
shaving creams and razors. Their

little shoes.
Their untied laces. While

a woman, always younger, behind them in a sundress
calls their names, at first so sweetly
before she's angry—and then
in panic:

Come back, come back. She'll have

a few sharp words to share if she can ever catch them—although
she knows also there will never, never, never be
any time for that. Those

boys continuing to run. Their
trembling chins. Their
little feet I loved and loved, and
would kiss again and again.

Beati mortui

Say: May they rest from their labors, these young men dying
        in countries far away.
Say: May their youthful naked bodies be lifted by assistants.
Say: May their sweetest childhood gardens be
        stuffed into bags and smuggled onto trains. May
            the pear trees be in bloom like ancient
                songs played on ancient instruments.

Say: May the gate swing open in this fairy tale to lovely girls, their legs
        bare, their bare feet stomping grapes. Say:

Secret pleasures enjoyed just once and then suppressed forever, returned
        to them. Say:

The wind has blown their fathers' checkbooks off the table. Say:

The weightless furniture of their mothers has been rearranged. Say:

Sugar glitters on the countertop. Restless shadows in an oven. Say:

An armless creature with antlers and a familiar face steps
        shyly off a page.

Room

There's a room inside myself
I've never seen.
There's

a bed there, and
on a nightstand, photographs
in frames. But

whose faces?

A violet
vase on a vanity: I've

held it in my hands. *Tearful
apology.* And

under my bed
in narrow boxes?
And if I open the desk
drawer, or
the dresser?

Well, just
the usual soft
folded things.
Silky
rectangles.
Knitted
squares.
A glove.
A stocking.

A loss, eternally.
And a window
(I'm sure of this)
that looks
out onto the green.
An apple tree.

And, beneath the tree, my
grandmother
in a housedress
in a lounge chair, sipping
a cool drink, not

even wondering
where she went or
where,
all these years,
she's been.

Masks

At the grocery store today—
these meteors and angels, wise men and all
the beautiful hallucinations of December, wearing
the masks of the Ordinary, the Annoyed, the Tired.
The Disturbed.
The Sane.

Only the recovering addict with his bucket and bell
has dared to come here without one.

He is Salvation.
His eyes have burned
holes in his radiance.
Instead of a mask, he has
unbuttoned his face.

Game

I thought we were playing a game
in a forest that day.
I ran as my mother chased me.

But she'd been stung by a bee.
Or bitten by a snake.
She shouted my name, which

even as a child I knew was not
"Stop. Please. I'm dying."

I ran deeper
into the bright black trees
happily
as she chased me: How

lovely the little bits and pieces.
The fingernails, the teeth. Even
the bombed cathedrals
being built inside of me.

How sweet
the eye socket. The spine. The
curious, distant possibility that God
had given courage
to human beings
that we might
suffer a little longer.

And by the time

I was willing to admit that
all along
all along
I'd known it was no game

I was a grown woman, turning
back, too late.

The Invalid

The meadow this morning
from the window
of the waiting room.
Rainy, April, and impatient:

Meadowless.
Can't see a thing.

Can only hear
the kind of music children
make with instruments
constructed
of wood and string.

Simple. Damp
wind.
An invalid
long ago
who grabbed my wrist:

Where do you think you're going
in such a pretty little hurry, Miss?

Lottery

Oh, we told you, we told you, the bolts wouldn't hold. And you, writing your opus on the air. And your mother, all those years on hands and knees in the backyard planting roses. And now your father openmouthed in a nursing home while the screen door blows open and closed (*the fucking latch is broken*) in some other hapless homeowner's fitful dream. Even your lovely son building temporary shelters for plastic men out of garden rocks. Oh, we told you, we told you, you and all of those you've loved.

And still somehow in the end, Daughter of the Lottery... you, with your sister the fruit fly muttering Psalm 23 in your ear... and the sky resonating in waves upon the sea... and the cool cross drawn on the brow of the melancholy child by a priest... and the bird in the mirror preening for the bird in the mirror preening.

Oh, we told you, we told you, as we traveled toward you, bearing your number through time and space—we shepherds and scribes waiting for you on your porch on another one of your short-sighted days:

The bolts won't hold.
The fucking latch is broken.
They'll die in feminine handfuls
on the earth, your precious roses.

And still. And still. And still, we couldn't help but be charmed by you. Watching your son in the garden with those rocks. The disposable camera held up to your eye. As if nothing could go wrong: "Not a cloud in the sky!" As if it could possibly go on and on. You and your endearing ignorance, your sweetly irrelevant bliss:

Okay, we admit it—the secret is that the world loves you in direct proportion to how much you love it:

You win.

Rondeau

Small and panting mass
Of moonlight and dampness on a log
This glistening tumor, terrible frog
Of moonlight and dampness on a log
My small and panting mass

Milk Tree

Heavy fruit
on bony branches
full of the knowledge one always encounters
too late
at the end of a life. Some

aspirin mixed with water, and a mouse
born in a dream. The sounds my son
once made while suckling. That, made
manifest. Little
milksop
and myself. Our

bodies, temporary
shelters, rented
breath. Not even
here long enough
to lament.

Today the breeze wears a fern:

Shiver
and living in the world, in
your brief green dress.

The amputated breast, like
a soul made out of flesh.

The Woman Escapes

Apparently
a mountainous sea
was moving its watery
trees toward me
so slowly
I couldn't see
until she
was purple shadows
and mountainous grandeur
in my front yard—

Ah, silent mother
asleep upon me
drowningly
loftily
endured
unheard
her heart
not beating
although
you know
by then
by then
(I cried
and tried
to explain to them)

it beat inside me,
it beat inside me

And at
the top of that
mountainous
fountain
a tree
with an eagle
with a pearl in its beak
and a turtle in a stream
gasping and breathing

A hare
A snare
A hart
Apart

And a bow
and an arrow
and a wildflower
and a nurse, distraught,
and a harried doctor
and a woman's shoes
too magical to lose
tossed in the water
burned on the pyre
lost in the closet
caught in the crossfire

And her coat, discarded
on the mossy path—
Think about *that*
Remember *that*
Recall how he scoffed:
You do the math
The chances

of this, the chances
of that
Your mother
and another
box of ashes—
her ashes
your ashes—
and how, flashing,
those last
days passed
climbingly
drowningly
Your answer
Your cancer
Don't laugh
You laughed
You laughed at that!

And then, there it was
It was
a mountain of
ocean,
a sharp wide sea
inside of me
inside of me
so wantonly
internally
at the core of me
and beyond me

Ah, fish in the flood!
Ah, poison in the blood
and a bird
like a word

from a tongue
taken flight
and, of course, every night

a wolf's silhouette
how predictable can you get
June and the moon etc.
Etc.

The love of a mortal
and the horror
of immortal
love
from a grave:
filthy dove
that won't move
from the window
or the pillow
stink
from the beak
shitting
on the rug:

you can pull the plug
and *still*
          I will
          love
my husband, my son,
my ugly
death
and my mangy, un-
domesticated pet
at the crest
of that wave

and a check
unwritten
on a mountain
of pharmacy
and fallacy

its worms
and forms
and the fury
of its insurance
agents
and impatience

with its filthy paws
and its wide-open jaws
and its head tossed back
and its howling

and it *is* howling
with all of its arts

or its gorging:
it's gorging
itself on its stars

Binoculars

This bird on the other side
of my binoculars—the cold life-light
around its mind, which was never
meant to be seen this clearly by a human being.
Still standing, decades later, in
a corridor, crying, having run from the room unable
to watch my mother die:
So there she is instead for the rest of my life. This
bird (my husband says it is a *flicker*) pretending
not to be staring straight back into my eye.

The Third Trumpet

On it, that beautiful tune
they like to play before the execution.
They played it through
the entirety of your life, but it
was background music.
You weren't supposed to listen to it.

And the food!
Spread out in bowls and baskets before you.
Mindlessly, you ate it
before the execution.

But the TV was on
and the children were shrieking.
No one actually expected you to chew it.

No. Only later. Some
might say *too late*.
Nostalgia on the way to the gallows.
That emperor's daughter, whose
beautiful name, *Nostalgia*, meant
gray ashes on the garden path.

But what day of a life is ever
not the day before the execution? And

what could be sweeter than these
first few hours of every season
wherein the wind
and the trees
and the tune of it, repeated, and

the shining body climbs
out of its hole
to crawl to the feast
on hands and knees
in its ruined uniform, perfumed?

A Dog, About to Pounce, Looks Back

This impulse to go, to stay, to rush
after it, and to turn away. This
life like the table
set for celebration
on a glacier melting a little more every day.
And candles to be lit on a cake, and
someone who has never been happier beside
someone who cannot bear
to look into the happy one's face.

And a park full of boys on skateboards
and old men on benches today.
And one mother parting the candles' flames
with her bare hands to search
for a child behind the science
and the saving. Look

at this mess! Surgical gowns and silver
instruments littering the floor of this place.
Your child's hand has turned into a mirror.
Your child holds a hand up to your face.

For the Young Woman I Saw Hit by a Car While Riding Her Bike

I'll tell you up front: She was fine—although
she left in an ambulance because
I called 9-1-1

and what else can you do
when they've come for you
with their sirens and lights
and you're young and polite
except get into their ambulance
and pretend to smile?

"Thanks," she said to me
before they closed her up. (They

even tucked
her bike in there. Not
one bent spoke on either tire.) But I

was shaking and sobbing too hard to say goodbye.

I imagine her telling her friends later, "It

hardly grazed me, but
this lady who saw it went crazy…"

I did. I was
molecular, while
even the driver who hit her did
little more than roll his eyes, while

a trucker stuck at the intersection, wolfing
down a swan
sandwich behind the wheel, sighed. Some-

one touched me on the shoulder
and asked, "Are you all right?"

(Over
in ten seconds. She
stood, all
blond, shook
her wings like a little cough.)

"Are you
okay?" someone else asked me. Uneasily. As if

overhearing my heartbeat
and embarrassed for me
that I was made
of such gushing meat
in the middle of the day
on a quiet street.

"They should have put *her*
in the ambulance, not me."

Laughter.
Shit happens.
To be young.
To shrug it off:

But, ah, sweet
thing, take
pity. One

day you too may be
an accumulation
of regrets, catastrophes.
A clay animation
of Psalm 73 (*But*

as for me, my feet…). No. It will be
Psalm 48: *They*

saw it,
and so they marveled; they
were troubled, and hasted away. Today

you don't remember the way
you called my name, so
desperately, a thousand times, tearing

your hair, and your clothes on the floor, and
the nurse who denied your morphine
so that you had to die that morning
under a single sheet
without me, in
agony, but

this time I was beside you.
I waited, and I saved you.
I was there.

THREE

That Men Should Kill One Another

Cecidit, cecidit Babylon

Twilight sprawls across her grave like a drunken lover, while
some pretty, melancholy
bird, ages past, sings *sadness
sadness* to the happy farmhand

and *be glad be glad* to the dying lamb.

Ah, the whole country is going
straight to hell again:

Old women are weeping on their way, dropping
handkerchiefs behind them on the path. Children pass
through empty rooms
wearing elaborate masks.

Recession, foreclosure, our
piety on fire. War
passing through the garden on its way to the parade.
She has fallen, Babylon the great. Such nakedness: in
our shattered mirrors, our jewel-encrusted faces.

The Book of Life

Pale and naked without their bodies, the souls
examine the book
in which they hope to find
their names inscribed.

Made of soap. Now. Made
of smoke. Now
made of dew
and hairlessness. And how

primitive, I realize, seeing them, it's been:
The body. Its

silly limbs transporting, through the world, our
windblownness. Our
cloud wherever it went.

Teeth, old-fashioned and enameled, so
easily chipped.
The nose, often
runny, sometimes broken.
Heavy eyelids. Ankle twisted. How

did we bear it as it bore us, all
stuttering and limping, clomping, hungry,
shaggy, horny, and diseased. All

that meat—grossly, morosely—weighted
around a soul:

A simple soul!
Exhausting coat!
Skipping along like hope.

Twentieth-Century Poetry

All that excited writing, a hundred years
passing like a child on a sled
down a hill in a blur
ending at the edge of a forest in which
unspeakable acts have occurred:

Suddenly, not a sign
of the child you were.

Not a footprint, not a whisper, not a word. Just

a certain dog made out of dusk. A certain
broken will. Some starlets

in the swimming pool, like water lilies floating in champagne.
The tiny bites
we took of things
too delicious to waste, and also the way
we devoured without tasting
those delicious, wasted things.

And here she comes, Poetry, walking
her wild creature on a leash.
Its eyes are a rabbit's eyes—crazy and pink—but

its beautiful coat is a mink's, and its
hard little horns are a goat's, and
its teeth gleam like moonlight on a tropical beach,
and its hooves:

You must look away
from those dainty, cloven things. Once
they belonged to the devil. Now

they are a beauty queen's bright feet.

Twentieth-century poetry—an eagle
in a cave, bleeding: such
a lot of noble suffering
in a dark and lovely place, full
of widows, pleading:

the torture, the tea, the briefly
held beliefs.
How swift, how gone it goes, completely. Everything
at once, like an eyelid
sliding closed
on a prophecy. Like

mouth, and boot, and songs
sung underwater. Someone's

knife blade on a freeway. Someone's
daughter.

Swans + dawn = *Good morning, babe.*
Wind + wronged = *Hurricane.*

How sad, the punctuation. Pound
in Pisa in a cage. In London
his friend Eliot
shaking a fountain pen.

How troubling, the random
torn-up pages
and the tattered flag being waved.

The Lover.
The Recluse.
The Mother.
The Martyr.
The Terrible Father.
The Farmer.
The Firebomber.

How calmly it all passed
in these photographs:

the sheep grazing
in the disease and the green, as if
some sweet thing had simply
dropped her parasol
into the sea, where it became
a little island
made of lace
and shade
obliterated in a dream.

Abel de Larue, 1582

A black spaniel appeared before him
and promised not to hurt him
provided he surrendered
himself to the dog

and kept this surrender a secret forever.

The impossible secret.
The impossible forever.
The vast, shuffling, gray migrations of surrendered
people crossing a plain

carpeted with ashes
disappearing into the shadows
of a forest long since burned to the ground.

The museum of ancient bloodstains.

The monastery quarantined during the plague.

Just try stifling the sounds of certain things.

Now, just a few of the billions who died before us
at home in their tiny shining places.

The Cure

He said, Take the scroll and eat it,
and it will make you sick.
Sicker than you've ever been, but with
the taste of sweetest honey on your lips.

Trust me, he said. I who, once, wearing
rubber gloves,
plucked the diamond from the mouth
of a lion. I who
once boiled
my own mother's
body down to the bones out of love.

Trust me, he said. He who had rowed
a thin boat
for thousands of years to get to this.
His name chiseled
in hieroglyphs. A fly on the shoulder
of his white coat
playing a violin.

Imagine, he said, as I have:

Imagine, you live
after having been
so carefully selected by death.
Your mother, your grandmother, their mothers'
mothers, the great gray owl waiting
for you at the gate:

her feathered breast.

Yes, I said. And all this foliage in the torso!
Trying to control it. Branches and leaves
through the mouth, the eye, the vagina,
the anus, *just say it:* With

a disease like this you can't be shy.

But imagine instead, he said, a light
so close and fierce it does
the opposite of blind you.
It floods you with sight, until
you are the chalice
bearing the fire.
You are the temple seven generations
died building around the idea of brightness.

Yes, please, I cried. More terror, more time, more—
For there shall be no night there.

(This catheter in your bladder, there will be
a plane crash when I yank it.)

(When I catch you in my net and pin you
to this piece of cardboard
with your wings spread
you will hear a woman gasp.)

Thank you!

You trust me, he smiled, he said…

He who once placed his own diamond
in the mouth of a lion in the name of science!

He who once boiled his own mother's
body down to the bones out of love!

Ten million human
experiments, experimenters, and I'd
watched some of them die
with my own eyes.
He also cried. He

fed me the pages, and I could taste
the blood in his boot prints and the way
a single thought might shine for
decades at the center of a mind.

Yes, he
was the man who smashed
the vase that had been placed
so carefully on my grave.
He was the man who silenced the music
at my funeral
being played.
He was the night

watchman
with a flashlight
and the soldier
on patrol
and the messenger
being sent
and the butcher
scouring the board
and the man
in the clock tower holding

time, laughing, back
by its hands. He

was—or
was he a woman?

A quiet woman. The woman
at the front desk who casually asked,
"How do you feel?" and sent me the bill
as if nothing's a particular miracle here.

             ongbirds
             my breasts
flustered
and sang
and ate me
for
forty-eight years, three
months, one week, six
days (a portion
for foxes, you
shake your head)
on my chest, and left
behind
these wrecked nests.

Comedy

It's a fine day
except for the doll
someone hung from the overpass.
We've all slowed down to gawk
at its awful nakedness, its
little black shoe, floppy bonnet, rope
tied around its neck.
If the cops don't get here soon

someone will have an accident.
Someone will have a heart attack.
Someone will get sued.

Everyone's a comedian:

The teenage boys somewhere
shoving a mannequin off a roof.
The medical students in a morgue
goofing around with a corpse.

Just a simple, bad, practical
joke. The sun's
rays,
luminous
alleys and passageways

leading to little dark places:

The heart, that industrial
center. The mind, that
tower with a sniper. How

much we hate
one another
is apparent in the laughter.
But something else in the braking and
the gasping. This

comedy, like
the cat staring aghast
at a parrot: *Jesus*

Christ, it thinks, *captured*
bird that speaks

the language of the Master.

Ativan

That dream of a cricket
in the dark of the night
at the foot
of the gallows tree.

Virtuous
cricket. Little, hopeful,
heart-
shaped face
lit up by the moon.

Little, hopeful, insistent
song
about the future
sung
to a hanged man's boots.

The Second Death

So like the slow moss encroaching, this
dark anxiety. In the bricks
by now
and all along
the shaded left side of the house.

And the statue, behind her knees. Her
ankle, in the cool
space between her breasts, spreading
in the earliest hours
of the morning.

Between her fingers.
Her parted lips.
That black-green
whispering.

The Common Cold

To me she arrives this morning
dressed in some
man's homely, soft, cast-off
lover's shawl, and some
woman's memory of a third-
grade teacher
who loved her students a little too much.
(Those warm hugs that went
on and on and on.)

She puts her hand to my head and says,
"Laura, you should go back to bed."

But I have lunches to pack, socks
on the floor, while
the dust settles on
the *I've got to clean this pigsty up.*
(Rain at a bus stop.
Laundry in a closet.)

And tonight, I'm
the Athletic Booster mother
whether I feel like it or not, weakly

taking your dollar
from inside my concession stand:

I offer you your caramel corn. (Birdsong
in a terrarium. Some wavering distant
planet reflected in a puddle.)

And, as your dollar
passes between us, perhaps
you will recall
how, years ago, we
flirted over some impossible
Cub Scout project.
Hammers

and saws, and seven
small boys tossing
humid marshmallows
at one another. And now

those sons, taller
and faster than we are, see
how they are poised on a line, ready
to run at the firing of a gun?

But here we are again, you and I, the
two of us tangled up
and biological: I've

forgotten your name, and
you never knew mine, but
in the morning
you'll find

my damp kisses all over your pillows,
my clammy flowers
blooming in your cellar,
my spring grass
dewed with mucus—

and you'll remember me
and how, tonight, wearing my
Go Dawgs T-shirt, I

stood at the center
of this sweet clinging heat
of a concession stand
with my flushed cheeks, and

how, before we touched, I
coughed into my hand.
Look:

here we are together
in bed all day again.

K—

Who lay unmoving
in his hospital bed
still running through a dream. And

the doctors whispered something
to the parents. Just

words. But irreversible. Like

the spell cast so long ago on the trees.

Outside Are the Dogs and the Sorcerers

August, all this
lost dog, sorcery
of cabbages in gardens, of
someone's steaming laundry, someone's

skull opened to an awful kiss, or poor prognosis. Someone

recites a charm, the dog comes home, the
surgeon drops a sponge, a nurse picks it up:
moist thought.

Oh, to be the swimmer in this humidity
whose body melts around him in the water
while he swims away from it today.

Midnight

At midnight the train conductor grinds the whole thing to a halt. All

the days in their separate cars crammed with the elementary particles
that would have made the hours possible
until dawn, and

the slow risings, and the washings, and

the hurried breakfasts, the many lunches
wrapped in silver foil, the old
complaints: *We're
out of paper towels. The cat got out. Where's my keys? We're going to be late.*

And the traffic jams.
And the weekend plans.

Now, He's stepped onto the tracks, sauntered off. The haunted

playground full of children. The oncologist. The postman. The woman
who agreed to do my taxes. I
call and call
out to them all
and no one answers.

The train's not moving, they whisper behind my back. *Her
conductor's gone.*

Gone:

He, who once cupped a cricket in his hands
and wouldn't open them until I'd paid its ransom.

He who, once, with a black Magic Marker, drew
a circle around my terror, laughed, and then
X-ed it out with a slap on the hand, a shot in the air, the memorized
words of a beautiful prayer:

Look. I took you this far, He whispers into my hair:

The middle of the night.
The middle of nowhere.

Beast of the Sea

And there was given to it a mouth with which to speak
great things and blasphemies. And there was given
to it, too, authority, and hierarchy, and
men and women worshiping.

This was the dream of that winter during which
I was told I might need to leave the world
with my son and husband in it.
I might have pictured

a cruise ship dragging emptiness over the Atlantic.
A cloud passing over it carrying a million minutes.

Cool slices of time set down before a man I'd never met.
And the woman I would never be.
Behind me, the indescribable. Such beauty. Ahead of me
memory—

That door to the enchanted village with
its bird-bearing trees. Seed
tossed into the future around which everything

is formed
eventually, whether
or not you're there to see it.

That beast, that
time-and-space machine.

FOUR

A Dog, About to Pounce, Looks Back

Beast of the Sea

His skin is spotted. His cloven hooves. His
hands and horns and diadems. His sea. Its
fluid wall of water and wind.
Its waves, its stars, its barges.
Its anchors sunk so deep they've become—

No one home.
The TV dreaming
in color behind
its blank screen.
Or the patient
after surgery:

something licking her wounds in her sleep.

I have been her, blinking
back into this world, while

something happened
and kept happening

but not to me.

Some terrible
national tragedy
unfolding. Or a kid

picking all the flowers in my garden
to give to me.

Oblivion

It is a cow standing there in that field
at the center of this meteor shower.
My father's teeth in a dish, and a little
jewelry box with a bit
of lightning in it. Closed lid. The future
movie star glimpsed
from the subway tracks by a rat. Wrist-
watch on a sunken ship on the captain's
wrist. The shining
nakedness inside
her gown
of the bride. At the bottom
of the watery cave, a single
neon fish. Such

stillness.
Complete.
And you, with
your head on a satin pillow in a box as they
wheeled you out of the church
(I watched it)
into the parking lot
(from my car).

May Morning

The thoughts of the schoolgirl dragging
her backpack across the grass.
The thoughts of the sleep-
walker, and the trashman, and
the flower tender, and the
teenage couple at the mall.

Like I have been handed them all.
Like I have heard their music, as

if the saints. The way
the lilacs that day. As if

a glass box of it. Like

a vial of perfume poured all
over the whole of creation—
perfume extracted from the sky.
Like no grammar.
No makeup.
No time behind my blindfold:

When the hospitalized child
stopped me in the hallway
and told me his name.
Sebastian.

His little white gown. His tiny smile. Blind-
fold yanked off after thousands of years.

Who needed eyes?

Fiftieth Birthday

Infatuation, that feathered whale. That
summer I was fourteen and wanted
a black eye longingly. Longed

for him to give one to me. If

only I were brave enough
to give one to myself. With
the telephone receiver. The encyclopedia.

And if *that* wasn't love…

Poor Mother, desperate
lullaby sung in a tunnel:
You're too young to be in love.

And you're too old! I screamed.
Older now than she'll ever be.
And tonight, this documentary:

washed up on the shore, the carcass
of some rotting, welcome beast.

Of the Dead White Men

Because some of them crawled on broken
hands and knees to save me
with their poems.

Because I was only
wretchedness at the edge of an abyss
of fashion magazines, and that

trickle of water down the side of their mountain
into my empty
cup, which I
refused to drink from: They

were offering that to me, although
I would not learn their statistics
or read their anthologies. Instead

I washed my face in their blood.
Instead I tossed my hours into their coffins.
Instead I was just some
obstinate dust rising from a lampshade.
My tatters in rags without them:

a girl blinded by her own hair
riding her bike somewhere—
stupid, dying for want
of what was written there. But

to them I remained a glittering
starvation, forgiven. Willing
to burn their hands for me

to deliver it, burning
while I denied
that it was burning.

I was like a child
outside a cave of snow
that had collapsed on her many fathers.
I laughed, wildly, for a little while.
And then I screamed.

And then I pouted.
And then

I grew older, and had to begin
to dig my own
pitiful little
hole with a teaspoon
to get them out again.

Tall Grass

for A

Consider the tall grass. Such
hope. Such confidence. How
a thing might spin itself
out of nothingness under
the ground, without

instructions, without words, with-
out any memory, sending

up this living thread. This
green breath to the surface. *Oh,*

bless it. Bless it. Where

finally, the wind, the laundry
on the line
rinsed blue by the sky. To have

come to it on such thinness *oh,*
please let the weather be mild. My
God, consider this:

The man who lost, and loved.
The woman who failed, and tried.
The polite
smile, at
his mother's funeral, of her child.

Helicopter

Middle of the night, hovering over.
Some bad crash near here on some back road?

Someone bleeding on a steering wheel
I suppose, while someone else is trying
to decide from the sky
where to land this
spectacular contraption.

Its wind
in the dark
thrashes over the trees
like Yahweh
over Egypt.
Like thieves rummaging through summery leaves.

Some mother's teenage son?
(Most likely drunk.)
Some bend in the road
he never saw coming?

And now
this monster-white flower made of sound
is coming down.
Is coming down.

Fantasy/Sci-Fi

The broom closet to another planet.
The impending planetary disaster.
The children in their maniac
trances. The rockets.
The neighbors. The
openmouthed spectators. The boy

tumbling into the bottomless well.
There, the cornstalks. The rooster
at the center of the earth.
And also on Mars.
Backward, the familiar landmarks.
And the plain voice
which spoke your name

in the middle of the night
on that long drive through Nebraska.
You just kept driving. What

else could you do? Slow down?

And your father who made you
by spilling his billion stars into the dark, while
crying out to your mother
as the sea washed her up on the shore
in the 1960s
with her long hair and her
vegetable recipes. And

you, small package of meat and dream.

And Beethoven, who lived
and died
deaf. Music.
Oblivion.
The kitten

named Sally, alive
for an hour. Then
dead, forever.

Dead forever.
Nowhere, the beginning.
Nowhere, the end.
Like ours, her eyes
never even opened. Like
her, do we

have any idea
where we are?
Where we were?
Where we're going?
Even yesterday?
Even today.

Christ Appears in a Mandorla Enclosed by a Cloud

And someone I love, pointing out a star, angrily, to me, "*That one.*" And then, to see it:

White bird flown into the windshield. A woman forcing an empty envelope into a man's empty hand. The way

someone on a telephone once insisted to me that all things happen for a reason. And

I found I could no longer speak, only listen, imagining this new existence. How

it took place in the air between us. How it was being knitted invisibly into invisible systems

by bitter old women, who nonetheless loved us, who wanted only what was best for us, and

knew exactly what that was.

Door

Broken door this morning
banging in the wind, like
someone who slammed it once
and stomped away
and wanted to be let back in:

Memory, and
longing, but
not this morning.

Not this morning, as I

lie unburdened in the
creeping sun, and think *Thank
God* my father's two years ashes, and
my mother so long and safely
dead and gone. All

over, all
over, their
embryonic unfolding, the
slow brass clock on their mantel, the
peaches they liked to savor in summer.

And our family jokes, our
secret passwords, their
hopeful faces, their
corn on the cob and their paper plates.

Thank God. *Thank God.*
Buried, burned, forgotten
where nothing else can harm them.

The Martyr's Motel

They'd traveled one by one
on their knees beneath the earth
to be gathered at the station
to be given robes and halos and official papers.

And a bus ticket each to the roadside motel
in Ohio that held
the reservations in their names, where
those who'd been slain before them were waiting.

Can these be the right martyrs? Can this be the place?

They rubbed their eyes as they pressed, to the bus
windows, their faces:

Everything was the same.
The familiar children splashing in the pool.
The barbecue.
The sound
of ice being dumped
into plastic buckets.

My God, we're
here again, out of all
the possible motels
in time and space?
Who

could have prepared them
for such homely terror? Even

after the eyes
gouged out and the necks severed, the hands
cut off and the racking wheel, how

such a simple, happy memory
captured in a snapshot
could mortally wound a martyr
long after the suffering was over.

The Accident

The Creator who dashed off a bird, who
snapped His fingers over the waters, and—
Holy shit. What is it?

A fish, He said. A lot
like a bird
except it swims.

He's so
talented, the other gods said of Him. But
that wasn't it. Like

the coffee of my subconscious spilled
all over my wedding dress, looking
down from such a distance:

What the poem must have looked like on the page
to the student assigned
to read it, who
could not read, and the way

it took me all semester
to understand what he was faking, because
the others, who
seemed to read, seemed
also not to understand.

Still, I should have guessed. Not
understanding made *them*
angry, while

He kept raising His hand to give me
better, stranger answers to my questions:

Consider daffodils.
Consider cancer.
Consider certain tiny lizards, and that

long before
anyone could count
there was still math.

Ivan

Our rooster's name is Ivan.
He rules the world.
He stands on a bucket to assist
the sun in its path
through the sky. He
will not be attending
the funeral, for God

has said to Ivan, *You*
will never be sick
or senile. I'll
kill you with lightning
or let you drown. Or

I'll simply send
an eagle down
to fetch you when you're done.

So Ivan stands on a bucket
and looks around:

Human
stupidity.
The pitiful
cornflakes in their bowls.
The statues of their fascists.
The insane division of their cells.
The misinterpretations
of their bibles. Their
homely combs—and,

today, absurdly, their
crisp black clothes.

But Ivan keeps his thoughts
to himself, and crows.

The First Resurrection

The moth locked up all
winter in the strongbox.
Mostly
mind after a while.
Flimsy scrap
of sky. Diligent
calm.

Like my father
without weight. The door

between us made of water.

Wake up, Daddy.
Your cup. I'm calling.
The whole

thing at once—once

and for all.

Recall the Carousel

Recall the carousel. Its round and round.
Its pink lights blinking off and on.
The children's faces painted garish colors against
an institutional wall. And the genetics. The
We won't be here too long... Do not step off...
The carousel? Do you recall? As if
we were our own young parents suffering again
after so many hundreds of hours of bliss.
And even the startling fact that
what had always been feared might come to pass:
A familiar sweater in a garbage can.
A surgeon bent over our baby, wearing a mask.
But surely you recall
how happily and for how long
we watched our pretty hostages go round.
They waved at us too many times to count.
Their dancing foals. Their lacquered mares. Even
a blue-eyed hunting hound
was still allowed back then.

Nine Herbs

after Bill Abernethy's translation of the
Old English charm

...

First you must recite this little charm nine times, and then...

...

Remember, Mugwort, what you told us?
What you arranged at Regenmeld for us?
Against poison, against contagion, against
the hateful one who travels through the land?

Three against thirty, Mugwort.
Remember? Remember

polio, tuberculosis, HIV?
Remember sickle cell and diabetes?
Pediatric cancers? Hemophilia?
Have you forgotten these?

And you, Waybread?
Mother of all herbs!
Over you, our carts
have creaked, our pigs
have snorted. Our
brides cried out in pleasure
or in pain, but
when we crushed
you, you
came to life again!

Please, Waybread, now,
holiest of all plantains:
The hateful one
has learned our names.
To you we pray.

And Watercress!
O Watercress.
Forget not our malignancies!
For the lesser shall be the greater
and the greater the lesser,
and so shall always be...
To you, who grows, like God on stone...

And you, dear Nightshade.
And you, our Chamomile.
You, Crab Apple. Lamb's Ears.
Wood Sorrell. Wallflower.
Fennel of the feathered leaves.

A worm came creeping
A worm came crawling,

And it tore a man in two...

A worm came creeping,
A worm came crawling,
But Woden, with a stick, hit
It, and it flew!

Hodgkin and Huntington.
Parkinson and Pick.
Gilbert, Graves, and Gehrig.
Kaposi, Bloom:

We curse your many sacred names!
We boil and blast and bathe and salve and sing!

Against red poison and reeking poison! Against the green
and yellow poisons, against the black poison, brown
poison, purple poison, blue. Against

water-blister and worm-blister,
thorn-blister and thistle-blister.
Against ice-blister
and north-blister.
Against west-blister,
fire-blister

from the south,
from the head,
from the stomach,
from the feet.

You must recite this charm of mine nine times, and then...

But to which pole can we flee
when it comes to us from each?

When it has videotaped our wives
at their ablutions? Photographed
our husbands as they mowed the lawn?

The do-gooders with the evildoers, we know.
The rich with the poor, of course.

But our dearest infants and oldest friends?
Our bitterest enemies, as well
as our teenage daughters in their scented beds?

And when, in the end, even
our sweethearts
turn from us
in sorrow
& disgust
you tell us to recite a charm, to grind
some herbs to dust? And if

this fails, what

then? *Then—*

...

First you must recite this little charm nine times, and then—

...

Atmosphere

No windstorm on the moon

Nothing ever moves

Childhood Sunday afternoons:

Just try to skip a stone across the waves
of one of those sad little February lakes:

Lake of the Library, Closed
Lake of So Many Bottles in the Basement
    that if you drink one or two
      no one will ever notice. Oh,
        only half a century later or so

I consider dialing the number
of my childhood telephone
just to see who's home:

But, I don't:

Little family

Sunday
Outside, snow

Too warm in the house
to wear a sweater
Nowhere to go

If it rings now, they'll
    also have to know:

All over
All over
No one will ever again be home

Leave them alone
Leave them alone

Over

Like the Stop sign after the windstorm, facedown on the wild ground.
Like forests without trees—no fires, no rapists, no killer bees.
Or, how lucky for us all that the moon was never found to be
made of diamonds or filled with gasoline. How easily, given

immortality, I could have been the little girl who peeled
all the petals from the peony
until only the suggestion of the peony was left. To be

the owner of the motorboat today
asleep in the cocktail lounge
while the waves crash against the lighthouse
and the Coast Guard searches for his corpse. The way

I once heard someone screaming *Relax! Relax! You're
not dying, asshole!* from the back of a passing ambulance.

Or the strange sight of a clown
on his back on a beach towel
as if the world is a game board, nothing more.
And this ant at the picnic confused inside my sandwich.
What now?

And the geese laughing over our heads.
And the crows in the branches.
And the branches themselves.
And the man in the Carhartt jacket long ago
who pulled over on the freeway to change my flat:

"Just go stand over there in that grass with your baby," he said.
"I got this for you, darlin'."

And I did, and he did, and forever after that...
And that's how my life passed...
I stood in that grass and sang, to my baby, a song...

Perfect all along.
The world, small and full of love.
And even better never to have understood this until now.

Present Perfect

This has been
the tiny house
in which we all
have, at one time, lived

in terror, in safety. History
has buried it.
Have wasted.

It has contained the wisdom
forbidden to us as children.
Little hand
has been slapped in an attic.

And the dark violet of some
summer night
in bed between
parents. The television

has glowed in our faces, and a car
has driven by outside, has built
rafters and pillars in the room
all around us

out of light. Has
brought them down.

Moved on.

Acknowledgments

These poems first appeared in the following journals:

The American Poetry Review: "Six Days" (as "Three Days")

Body: "Canto One"

Cheat River Review: "The Invisible Passenger"

Court Green: "Binoculars"

FIELD: "Present Perfect"

Granta: "The Common Cold," "The First Resurrection," "The Woman Escapes"

The Harvard Advocate: "Of the Dead White Men"

The Literary Review: "Midnight," "Room"

New England Review: "The Accident," "At the End of the Text, a Small Bestial Form," "Nine Herbs," "Perspective"

The Paris-American: "A Dog, About to Pounce, Looks Back," "K—"

Phoebe: "Beast of the Sea" ("When I realized" and "This morning the shadow"), "Masks," "That Men Should Kill One Another"

Ploughshares: "The Martyr's Motel"

Poetry: "Ativan," "Game," "In This Order," "Mushrooms," "Recall the Carousel," "Rondeau," "The Second Death," "You've Come Back to Me"

Post Road Magazine: "For the Young Woman I Saw Hit by a Car While Riding Her Bike"

The Southern Review: "The Cure"

Willow Springs: "The First Trumpet"

"Atmosphere," "For the Young Woman I Saw Hit by a Car While Riding Her Bike," and "Nine Herbs" were published in *House to House* (2013), a chapbook by Likewise Books. I am particularly grateful to the editor, Kylan Rice.

"Perspective" was republished in *The Best American Poetry* 2013.

Some of the titles, section titles, and poems' subjects and images were taken from or inspired by the Metropolitan Museum of Art's facsimile of *The Cloisters Apocalypse*, and from Jeffrey M. Hoffeld's commentary on the pages of the facsimile.

I am also eternally grateful to my editor, Michael Wiegers.

About the Author

Laura Kasischke has published nine previous collections of poetry and nine novels. She has been the recipient of the National Book Critics Circle Award and the Rilke Award for her collection *Space, in Chains,* as well as a Guggenheim Fellowship, two grants from the National Endowment for the Arts, and a United States Artists Award. Her fiction has been widely translated, and three of her novels have been made into feature-length films. She grew up in Grand Rapids, Michigan, and attended the University of Michigan, where she is now Allan Seager Collegiate Professor of English. She lives in Chelsea, Michigan, with her husband and son.

Editor's Circle

The Editor's Circle is comprised of distinguished patrons of the arts who express their dedication to poetry through their generosity and commitment to the prosperity of Copper Canyon Press. Each publishing season the Editor's Circle selects one forthcoming book that represents their shared appreciation of a poet whose work meets the highest standards of creativity and literary accomplishment.

Poetry is vital to language and living. Since 1972, Copper
Canyon Press has published extraordinary poetry from around
the world to engage the imaginations and intellects of readers,
writers, booksellers, librarians, teachers, students, and donors.

WE ARE GRATEFUL FOR THE MAJOR SUPPORT PROVIDED BY:

THE PAUL G. ALLEN
FAMILY FOUNDATION

Lannan

amazon.com

THE MAURER FAMILY
FOUNDATION

the
P INT

ART WORKS.

National
Endowment
for the Arts
arts.gov

golden
lasso

WASHINGTON STATE
ARTS COMMISSION

Anonymous

John Branch

Diana Broze

Beroz Ferrell & The Point, LLC

Carolyn and Robert Hedin

H. Stewart Parker

The Seattle Foundation

The dedicated interns and faithful volunteers
of Copper Canyon Press

To learn more about underwriting Copper Canyon Press titles,
please call 360-385-4925 ext. 103

The Chinese character for poetry is made up of two parts: "word" and "temple." It also serves as pressmark for Copper Canyon Press.

This book is set in two contemporary transitional typefaces. The text is set in Whitman, developed from Kent Lew's studies of W.A. Dwiggins's Caledonia. The heads are set in Mrs Eaves, designed by Zuzana Licko from her studies of Baskerville. Book design and composition by VJB/Scribe. Printed on archival-quality paper.